INTP: 33 Secrets From The Life of an INTP

By Diana Jackson

Contents

INTP: Introverted, Intuitive, Thinking and Perceiving

1. Usually societal thinkers and pioneers

Positive: INTPs, as societal thinkers and pioneers, might not always be the most interactive people in a group, but they are observing closely – oftentimes without even realizing it. Societal or social thinkers are highly adept at relating to others, or seeing others' points of views, and combined with INTPs' knack for creativity and forward-thinking, it makes them excellent problem-solvers in social situations – the one who uses logic to calm down a restless mob ready to grab their pitchforks.

Negative: The downside to this is that INTPs may be seen as bossy know-it-alls, and others might view them as the kind of people who get in the middle of others' arguments and make matters even more complicated or complex. INTPs do like to prove their brilliance in social situations (actually, in any situations), even if the other parties would rather they stay out. And INTPs might not always get that their interference isn't welcome.

In Relationships: It's a funny paradox that a personality type which can logically and efficiently solve others' problems are at a bit of a loss when it comes to their own personal lives. Relationships can be tough for INTPs, especially relating emotionally to their partner, but thanks to their intuitive and perceiving aspects, they are open to more creative forms of relationship 911 if things go south. The therapy simply has to satisfy their thinking aspect and make sense.

At Work: Like most introverted and intuitive types, the INTP can be a bit of a lone wolf on the job, but they are adept at managing social situations, such as they might come across in the workplace, where arguments and disagreements are common among squabbling coworkers. INTPs will come up with creative and effective ways of mitigating the drama, suggesting truces between coworkers that turn into lasting peace and keep the workplace busy and efficient.

2. Seeks to improve the things in their own environment

Positive: INTPs look at life as a constant work in progress, and they treat it as a dynamic environment where nothing is set in stone – everything can be made better. This makes them exceptionally ambitious and determined, the kinds of people who achieve and then overachieve, but, even better, the rest of the world tends to benefit from their hard work, receiving the positives in the professional, recreational, artistic and cultural arenas.

Negative: While it's definitely a good trait to want to leave things better than you found them, others can perceive this characteristic as something quite else – nit-pickiness. In fact, many people around the INTP, especially those closest, might feel as though nothing they do is ever good enough. Or others will look at them and think, "I must be a failure because I'm not doing as well as that person." It can be defeating or even drum up hostility.

In Relationships: If there is one place that the INTP's desire for constant improvement can be especially beneficial, it is in their relationships, particularly where the material aspects are concerned. That is to say, partners of the INTP will benefit from their mates' constant desire for bigger and better things, whether it's nice homes, fancy cars or beautiful clothes and jewelry. INTPs aren't materialistic or flashy by nature, but they do like good-quality things in their lives.

3

At Work: The INTP can be a bit off-putting in the professional world because of their lack of polished social graces, but any employer who can see past that will love their INTP employee, who certainly views their work as part of their immediate and important personal environment. This can include not only their workspace, which might be messy while making incredibly good use of the area, but also their actual projects, reports, etc.

3. Prefers to live inside their own mind and ignore the outside

Positive: We all know that listening too much to or caring too much about what others think is a recipe for lost identity or loss of focus. INTPs are in no danger of being distracted by others hating on them or trying to get them to change because they are focused on what is inside their own brain. For them, their own individuality and their personal brand of originality is what's important.

Negative: Sometimes, though, we need to press outside of our own thoughts. To be well-rounded individuals who can relate on a number of topics or feelings, or even to introduce new ideas that might spark some innovation, we have to listen to others and consider what they are saying with seriousness and due respect. INTPs will always have to make the effort to step outside of their own brains if the truly want to change the world.

In Relationships: As if it's not enough that INTPs are introverted to begin with, they can also end up taking their partners' presence for granted when they withdraw into their own minds. INTPs must always make sure that they are reaching out to the ones they love on a regular basis and not neglecting their spouses or families for the work that can consume them if they let it. If they're not careful, they will push away the people who care for them.

5

At Work: INTPs know they are quite brilliant at times, and that knowledge can make it easy for them to assume that no one else at their place of work has anything better to offer – so they shut them out. But that is where they are wrong, and INTPs would do well to keep in mind that no man is an island. They must tone down the arrogance and adopt a more welcoming personality, one that is open to the fluid exchange of ideas.

4. Very adept at analyzing difficult situations

Positive: Situations can be professional, social or personal, but the INTP, whose strong thinking aspect has them covered in terms of logical assessment, can take on all of them, at the same time, and still come out triumphant. They are simply good at making sense of things, good at connecting the dots, and their intuitive aspect works hard here as well, especially in situations where the relationship between a bunch of different parts might not be so obvious.

Negative: One of the unfortunate aspects of a normally positive personality trait like this is that you can start to go looking for situations to analyze, when in fact, what you see is what you get – you don't have to delve any further under the surface. Again, INTPs can sometimes take something quite simple and, by virtue of their dogged pursuit of the truth, end up with a messier, more complex result. INTPs have to learn to leave well enough alone.

In Relationships: On the one hand, being able to discover the root of a problem in relationships is incredibly useful – from there, you can strategize a solution and fix whatever ails you. However, INTPs aren't naturally emotional people, so their solutions are going to be less about the heart and more about the head – and if they're dating a feeling personality, this can lead to unresolvable friction that is simply the result of two totally different points of view.

At Work: Coworkers of the INTP might not like to admit it, but their know-it-all officemate has that distinction for a reason, and it can be easier sometimes to just accept that the INTP is going to gloat a little when they solve the problem first. It's just who they are, but more importantly, it's what they do, so whether it's an argument that has stretched on for too long or a project issue on the micro-level that needs to be fixed, the INTP is on it.

5. Identifies different patterns within their environment

Positive: A lot of the world is governed by patterns, and the INTP has a natural flair for discovering them and then turning them to their advantage. This makes them a precise and accurate sort of person, the kind of individual who impresses by showing up just the right amount of early (they know, after all, how to time their vehicle to hit all the green lights along the route).

Negative: If you have seen the movie *A Beautiful Mind*, starring Russell Crowe, it's easy to understand how the constant processing of patterns can make a person rather, ah, difficult to be around. It's like they are lost within their own world, a world that isn't relatable to feelings or emotions – just science and cold facts. If pattern-searching becomes a habit for the INTP, they can quickly become engulfed.

In Relationships: It might not be the most tactful thing in the world when the INTP tells his partner that she always gets a little more intensely emotional around a certain part of the month, but sometimes these facts and patterns need to be spoken. As long as it doesn't become a constant – as long as it stays out of the realm of the obnoxious – this trait can actually be very enlightening for couples.

At Work: Their ability to recognize patterns (the way some might recognize emotions) often has at least some influence on the field where the INTP works. This includes science and mathematics (INTPs make excellent mathematicians or physicists), but it can also include more literary or artistic pursuits – a well-crafted character in a novel must display persistent personality traits in order to seem realistic, while paintings rely on patterns of size and color to achieve satisfying harmony.

6. Comes up with logical explanations for the things around them

Positive: Much of the doings and happenings in the world around us can be explained logically, as long as someone is around who understands the science behind it. This is usually the INTP, and their ability to help people understand why things work the way they do goes a long way toward eradicated junk science, superstition and jumping to conclusions.

Negative: The fact is, people can only listen to someone who loves the sound of their own voice so much – after a while they start to tune them out. Unfortunately, when INTPs are particularly around people they know and trust, they can get in the habit of pontificating on the whys, even when no one asked in the first place, and it can be quite alienating (to say nothing of, well, dull).

In Relationships: Poor INTPs can have a really hard time relating to the people they love, and sometimes their partners and families – especially if they are feeling personalities – can be left utterly bewildered by their INTP's "take" on matters that are purely emotional. Sure, it makes sense that a wife is upset because she sees her husband look at other women, knowing full well he would never cheat...but it doesn't always help the situation to point that out.

At Work: If the INTP works in a science lab or in an office where their job is to develop ideas that can be turned into working machines, then their ability to stress logic is a total boon. In fact, it can be what sets them apart from all the others, ensuring that they receive recognition and commendation for all their hard work, simply because it stands out as the best in the company.

7. May seem aloof

Positive: If there is one thing that aloof people rarely have to deal with, it's other people asking them for annoying favors. The INTP might not actually be an aloof human being, but they don't mind appearing so if it keeps people they'd rather not talk to well at bay. Outwardly they are maintaining that snooty sneer, but inwardly they are giggling at how simple it is to avoid unwanted attention.

Negative: Aloofness (or perceived aloofness) can, however, lead to missed opportunities. If you seem unapproachable, then that timid neophyte – who wouldn't dare go up to the lofty INTP at a dinner party – will never have a chance to share the idea that would push the INTP's latest project into the realm of possibility. And when that happens, everyone loses.

In Relationships: If only life were more like Pride and Prejudice, where Mr. Darcy's aloof reserve eventually melts away as he falls headlong in love with Elizabeth Bennett. As it is, few people will be interested in penetrating the cool stand-offishness of the INTPs demeanor, but someone will come along who is up to the task – and they will find underneath a reserve of warmth, humor and delicious wit. INTPs just can't expect love to come easily.

At Work: Hopefully the INTP gets thrown into a work environment where no one will stand for their snooty attitude, and they will be given the room to come out of their shell and become more of a team player. Change is never easy, and while newbs might always be initially intimidated by the aloof-seeming INTP employee, the better they get to know one another, the friendlier and more humorous the INTP will become.

8. Has a tendency to lean toward skepticism

Positive: Snake oil might be a thing of the past, but con men and women haven't gone anywhere, and they have updated and modernized their strategies (Liberian lottery in your inbox, anyone?). The INTP is hardly going to give these scams a second glance, and even when it comes to more convincing information – scientific ideas, for example – if it sounds too good to be true, the INTP knows it probably is.

Negative: Have you ever watched a movie with someone who kept nudging you throughout, saying, "Ugh. That would NEVER happen in real life." They can be a bit of a pill, no? Well, that's the INTP for you, the guy or gal unwilling to suspend their disbelief for even a second, especially during those moments when doing so would bring them a lot of delight or entertainment. INTPs need to learn to just go with the flow sometimes, or risk missing out.

In Relationships: On the one hand, a healthy dose of skepticism is a good thing when it comes to new relationships – falling headlong in love with a stranger has its dangers (such as being manipulated, used and left). But the INTP will have to work at keeping their skepticism at bay the longer they are with someone, because constant doubts are a death knell to healthy coupledom. The right partner certainly helps, one who is warm, affectionate and unfailingly sincere.

At Work: While the INTP might be the person at work that everyone expects to nay-say a coworker's project proposal (Every. Single. Time.), their skepticism, if they work in the realm of science, is absolutely essential to the field. If medicine, for instance, was filled with a lot of yes-men doctors, we'd have hardly any effective cures. Only because there are people who doubt and demand better do we send people into space and eradicate cancerous cells from organs.

9. Puts a very high value on intelligence/ intelligent thinking

Positive: The intellectuals of the world have brought us math, sciences and poetry. They have made it possible for us to drive cars, hold tiny computers in our hands and call them phones and view movies that make us think long after the lights have come back on. So it's no wonder that INTPs value intelligence and intellectual thought above most else, because it is exciting, stimulating and inspirational; one intelligent idea almost always leads to another.

Negative: There are a lot of different kinds of intelligence out there, but the INTP might always recognize them. They recognize the kind that comes from an impressive college pedigree, a high IQ and perfect SAT scores. But that means they might fail to appreciate the mechanical intelligence that the greasy, sweaty guy at the garage has – the guy who doesn't wear a suit and tie but makes it possible for the INTP to drive their car to work every day.

In Relationships: INTPs might dabble in dating good-looking airheads, but they'll never settle down with them. They simply put too much stock in ambitious intelligence to ever consider spending the right of their lives with someone who considers gossip magazines or fluffy best-sellers to be engrossing literature. In fact, it might do for the INTP to date someone a little bit smarter than they are; that way, they will understand what it is to aspire to be with someone, rather than deign.

At Work: Although the perceiving aspect keeps most INTPs from seeking out positions that require a commitment to boring administrative tasks and well-established workplace hierarchies, they are nonetheless born to be professionals because they are drawn to careers that utilize their unique combination of forward-thinking creativity and practical logic. They don't want to just "do a job" – they want to be intellectually excited, challenged and given the opportunity to make a difference.

10. Not prone to strong displays of emotion

Positive: Some situations call for a poker face – for instance, during actual poker games, while shopping for a new car or during an open house. Keeping one's emotions tightly suppressed means that the INTP will come out the winner, and the seller who was willing to let their beachfront bungalow go at a knock-down price will have no idea just how much the cool-as-a-cucumber INTP was jumping up and down with thrilled excitement as the papers were signed.

Negative: Thanks to their thinking aspect, INTPs – like other thinkers – can come across as inhuman at times because of their lack of emotional display. Bear in mind, it's not that INTPs don't feel – they just don't see the point in showing it, because to their thinking, it makes things unnecessarily complicated and much worse than if the situation was not filled with tears or outbursts of anger. Not everyone sees it that way, though, and INTPs can cause a lot of unintentional mixed signals.

In Relationships: It takes a strong, secure and independent partner to make it work with the INTP, because they are not going to get a lot of feedback out of their mate. INTPs would do well to match up with people who have the patience to draw them out of their shells and get them to be more expressive, while making the effort to communicate their feelings when something is bugging them or when something has made them extremely happy.

At Work: If there is one good thing about the INTP's lack of emotional display in the workplace, it's that when something or someone is really getting on their nerves, everyone will know. Like a pop bottle that has been shaken a hundred times before someone finally comes along, takes the lid off and causes an enormous eruption, the INTP will make a hugely epic impression once they can no longer hold in their feelings.

11. Takes joy in some of the more obscure things in life

Positive: You don't always need a crowd to enjoy an activity – in fact, sometimes too many people is a bad thing. This is why INTPs will gravitate toward more obscure past-times and interests, as it pleases their introverted aspect and makes them feel even more special than they already are. And it doesn't end with hobbies – INTPs have an uncanny knack for appreciating small moments in life that others might not give a second thought to.

Negative: The downside to this interest in the obscure is that it can be rather isolating. As introverts, INTPs already would rather work on their own, so wanting to spend their leisure time as solitary individuals means that they aren't going to have many opportunities to meet new people, and if they do end up at a party or dinner, they will have a tough time finding common ground. No surprise that they leave thinking, "I was better off staying at home."

In Relationships: If INTPs can find mates who share in their joys and their interests, it will go a long way in opening them up to people who would love them and be there for them through thick and thin. INTPs already have a sense that they are destined to find someone truly special, so when that person comes along who also loves both the way dust dances in sunlight and really underground conspiracy theories, well...it's a match made in heaven.

At Work: So maybe your INTP coworker won't be the type to get all revved up over the Super Bowl (like everyone else in the workplace), but those rare and absolutely priceless emotional outbursts that come so infrequently may be brought out by something happening on the job – a problem that was solved through non-traditional means or even the building cafeteria starting to offer their favorite dish on Fridays. Even if no one else quite "gets it," everyone is happy to see the INTP happy.

12. Does not like rules

Positive: It might be surprising that someone who appreciates the logical application of math and sciences tends to reject the rules that govern our social spheres, but that is the INTP's perceiving aspect hard at play, and it's part of what makes this personality type so interesting. As a rule-bender, the INTP defies both conventions and expectations, and it gives this personality type a rather defiant air that others can relate to and admire.

Negative: Sometimes rules are in place for good reason, though, and while the INTP will follow the scientific method to the letter of the law, he or she will resent the larger social hierarchy that imposes order and prevents chaos in society. This can keep the INTP from being successful both on the job and in their social lives, because even something as simple as waiting your turn in line at the coffee bar can come with direct and unpleasant consequences if the rules are ignored.

In Relationships: INTPs often inhabit professional careers, so it might be shocking that in their relationships they are much more relaxed about titles and even traditional forms of fidelity. Pick your jaw up off the ground when you learn that your INTP friend is okay with not getting married after a dozen years with the same person or that they have experimented with an open relationship. No one is going to tell the INTP what he/she can or cannot do in their relationship.

At Work: INTPs can be difficult in the workplace, particularly if the company they work for thrives on a bureaucratic structure which ensures that everyone is but a rung on the corporate ladder. INTPs might not necessarily lead an out-and-out rebellion for change, but their unhappiness can manifest itself in a slew of disgruntled letters to HR or a series of petitions for greater workplace equality and freedoms. Being told to sit in one place and stay there for nine hours will not a happy INTP make.

13. Enjoys science fiction and fantasy

Positive: Science fiction and fantasy done right are exceptionally smart and entertaining. They are full of ideas about the future (which vastly appeals to the INTP's intuitive aspect) and may even make sharp social commentary about the present. The INTP's interest in these realms, whether it's Game of Thrones or Star Trek, is one area where this introverted personality type can find common ground with people they might not normally talk to.

Negative: Like anyone who can get stuck inside their own head, INTPs can have a tendency to overdo it on the things they love, and if that happens to include the ultra-sophisticated world of fantasy and sci-fi, well, they can bypass "superfan" level and go straight to "crazed and obsessed." This normally logical and practical personality type could end up sinking hundreds, if not thousands, of dollars into their favorite fandom.

In Relationships: As mentioned, their love of sci-fi and fantasy books, TV, comics, whatever, can make the less-open INTP more sociable and relatable, and it could be through this avenue that they meet someone with whom they end up sharing the rest of their lives. All it takes is one shared interest to bring two people together in conversation – and from there, the rest is history, as it opens the door to finding other similarities.

At Work: The same applies in the workplace, where at least the introverted INTP can get in on coworker conversations with an astute observation that no one else thought of. Further, great science fiction and fantasy are vehicles of inspiration, and the INTP is absolutely the sort of person who will introduce a new idea on the job and, after being lauded for brilliance, admit, "I read something similar in a book and thought it would work here."

14. Tends to have a difficult time expressing their feelings

Positive: One of the positives of delaying emotional expression is that where others are quick to unload their feelings – say, in a fit of anger or spite – the INTP gives him or herself enough time to stop and assess the situation. While it's not a purely strategic move – it really is because they don't know quite what to say – in the long run it can be more effective at maintaining peace. It certainly keeps them from saying things they'll regret later.

Negative: Sometimes, though, being able to express one's feelings is a necessity when you want a situation to change or to move forward. The INTP's inability to articulate how he or she feels can hold them prisoner, stuck in one place, in all aspects of their life: work, family, society. INTPs should recognize, though, that speech is just one form of communication; if they are good writers, they could choose to interact through heartfelt emails or letters.

In Relationships: It can be incredibly difficult for both the INTP and his/her partner to maintain good lines of communication, but it is absolutely essential for the health of their relationship that they do. So the INTP and the partner must find a middle ground or a compromise, and the INTP has to learn that opening up about one's feelings does make one vulnerable, but it also opens the pathway toward true intimacy and understanding.

At Work: INTPs tend to keep their heads down at work, happy to be doing what they love with minimal interruptions. This informs where they end up usually, because they won't be as likely to accept a job where the environment calls for a lot of collaboration – collaboration that could result with them having to state their will and then impose it upon others. INTPs work best when they are independent and unhampered by their own emotions and others'.

15. Can seem scattered or unorganized

Positive: INTPs can have a bit of an "underdog" persona going for them, as many introverts do (simply because they are not as outgoing as their extraverted counterparts). Their perceiving aspect also makes them appear to be disorganized and scatter-brained, but that's only what it looks like from the outside. INTPs are capable masters of controlled chaos, and they dare you to underestimate them – it makes their victory that much sweeter.

Negative: Many of us can manage quite well in a state of prolonged controlled chaos, but if INTPs are not careful, it will get away from them and they'll end up as frazzled as they appear to be. They walk a fine line between crazy and genius, and the line can get finer (or fuzzier) still as they get older and more set in their chaotic ways. A good personal assistant or partner can be instrumental in keeping INTPs on track.

In Relationships: The INTP's partner knows that deep down their mate is capable and responsible, and he or she cares deeply about the people they love. But that doesn't always make the responsibilities of home life easy, because while the INTP knows he or she has to do the dishes and sweep the floor (they didn't forget), the actual act can go unfinished for days. Anyone who has been in a live-in relationship knows that this can be insanely stressful for a couple.

At Work: The INTP desk might look like a disaster, but no worries – this personality type has things on lock. When their work is truly important to them, they are not going to forget where a significant document is lying, even if it's hidden under stacks of folders. INTPs do need to work on communicating their ideas more effectively, however, because what makes sense in their heads doesn't always translate when it comes out of their mouths.

16. Awkward in social situations with unknown people

Positive: Awkwardness in social situations can go two ways, but you always hope for the one where the INTP's awkwardness is actually endearing, and they get started on a subject that is interesting to others, while getting animated and excited without realizing it. Awkwardness can also work in the INTP's favor because they won't be inundated with people trying to strike up conversation – giving them plenty of time to survey the room and take in their surroundings.

Negative: If only everyone could be that clever, witty person who easily converses with strangers and makes friends wherever they go. Unfortunately, that is not the INTP, and he or she will need just the right environment in order to shine in a social situation. The other 99.99 percent of the time, the INTP can come across as kind of weird, not very personable and slightly "off." Those who know the INTP love them, but everyone else is going to be a bit wary.

In Relationships: INTPs would do best to stick with other introverts when it comes to their mates, but the occasional extravert will come along and just rock their world. The INTP will find him or herself unable to avoid social situations and may make the effort, for the sake of the one they love, to be more outgoing. This, in turn, could end badly (or humorously, depending), but at least they tried.

At Work: INTPs who are established in their position and have known their coworkers for years will go about their day happily, but those who are new to a job might have a tougher time blending in at first. It just takes time. During company social functions or business trips they might not be the best people to use as the face of the company, but they make excellent behind-the-scenes magicians and fixers, ensuring that presentations go smoothly.

17. Very sure in their own values and thinking, not easily persuaded

Positive: There are a lot of wishy-washy people out there who are subject to the thoughts and ideas of others, and who are willing to change their own beliefs to match that of their friends' or their mates'. But not the INTPs, who don't go out of their way to make a big deal out of their beliefs, but who nonetheless hold steadfast to them, with an unshakeable sense of personal righteousness.

Negative: Self-assurance and confidence in one's beliefs can be easily misconstrued as arrogance, and in the case of the INTP, it can often lead to "fingers-in-the-ears" syndrome, where they are unwilling to listen to others' perspectives. It's almost as if they are afraid to hear someone else and accept that that person's idea is better or more logical. If INTPs can be charged with a deadly sin, it's the one of pride.

In Relationships: It can be very appealing for others to find someone who truly has a good sense of who they are. If INTPs can be a bit awkward around people, at least they can speak on the topic of their own beliefs with authority and assuredness, which can go a long way in impressing a mate. They will also want to be sure they pass on these beliefs to their children and will look for partners with similar thoughts.

At Work: INTPs must learn to keep their minds open to the thoughts and beliefs of others in the workplace, because it is truly one location where collaboration is, ultimately, essential. But their dogged adherence to their own values – however traditional or nontraditional they may be – means that the INTP is at least consistent, if not predictable at times. If they can tap into their perceiving aspect's open-mindedness in the workplace, the INTP can be infinitely more productive.

18. Likes unusual things/people

Positive: As introverts, INTPs might not be expected to mix with crowds of people, but the people with whom they do mix are often eclectic and unusual. INTPs are creative and surprisingly spontaneous, open to new ideas and easy-going with people they know well, so they are at their comfortable best when in small groups, among fascinating people, talking about interesting, taboo-pushing topics. There's a lot no one knows that lurks beneath the INTP's surface.

Negative: If INTPs come across as socially awkward and weird, it could be because they are interested in things that might not have a place in standard, public conversation. Forced to chit-chat about mundane topics like the weather and the price of gas, INTPs can appear to be bored out of their minds – which, indeed, they likely are, and they are counting down the minutes until they can get back to the people and things they truly enjoy.

In Relationships: If the INTP scientist, for example, shows up at a company Christmas party with his or her mate, everyone else might be a bit surprised at how much of an "odd couple" they appear to be. But actually, the INTP wears something like a mask while in the professional world, and they let their hair down at home, filling their house with unusual artifacts or artwork and dating people who might look alternative or nontraditional.

At Work: If they can, perceiving INTPs will happily accept a job that pays less money but offers more personal freedoms and places them among free-spirits who value the same. This can mean they work among a mish-mash of "misfits" or that they do work that lies outside of the boundaries of "normal" professional work (think of a private detective career, for instance). INTPs also find contentment studying and creating things that have never been studied/created before, like extremely specialized scientific research.

19. Actively seeks to either prove or disprove existing theories

Positive: The mind of the INTP never stops, and they are always looking for an intellectual challenge. While their extraverted counterpart might prefer to actually get into it with other live human beings, the INTP is not as confrontational and prefers to "have it out" with existing theories. This is part of what makes them such able scientists, though they apply it to all aspects of their lives as they attempt to clean-up the world by filling it with truth.

Negative: On the downside, INTPs sometimes need to know when to quit – and they often don't. No matter how petty the theory, the INTP is like a dog with a bone, and he or she will pursue the truth of the matter with a single-mindedness that is both astonishing and a little crazy. INTPs need to calm down and realize that they don't always have to be right and they don't always have to try to "fix" things.

In Relationships: If the partner of the INTP feels as though they are taking part in a live study, it's because they technically are. The INTP has a lot of ideas about how relationships work, and instead of just letting love happen, they are going to be a little different about it. On a more micro level, expect the INTP to argue their POV or opinion to the death, because they truly believe it to be the "right" one.

At Work: Yet in a scientific laboratory or a research study, this quality is an absolute boon. The only reason we have computers and TV and cars and medicine – and the only reason they get better and better, each year – is because people like the INTP are constantly questioning the norm, re-testing it and re-assessing it for how it could perform better. Under their watch, a theory which is almost there, but not quite, will not see the light of day until it is perfect.

20. Extremely intelligent

Positive: Extreme intelligence is what makes the world's technologies progress, and the INTP is at the forefront of the forward-moving motion. They are not just smart – they are usually quite brilliant, and they're apt to shine in whatever professional field they have chosen, as well as impressing their friends and families with their effortless ability to think up creative and effective ideas, like how to handle a multi-family Christmas so that everyone is happy.

Negative: INTPs are extremely intelligent – and they know it. And this can make them rather snooty and arrogant when dealing with people that they perceive to be less intelligent. INTPs should keep in mind that their intelligence, while extremely useful, can drive a wedge between them and the rest of society if they let it. There's just no substitute for kindness and understanding, no matter how many complex math problems you can solve.

In Relationships: As highly intelligent individuals, INTPs are definitely going to settle down with someone who is a match for their brains. They might try dating a dim-witted beauty or stud, but it won't last – their need for intellectual conversation and common interests is too strong, and they want someone with whom they can constantly share ideas, as well as children and a home and all that other good stuff.

At Work: It's interesting that INTPs are so smart, because their perceiving aspect can work against them to derail it. INTPs would thrive in corporate positions were it not for their perceiving aspects, which utterly rejects the bureaucracy within a tall office building. Yet INTPs are so smart, they can figure out how to make a living doing something that isn't soul-sucking and doesn't require a suit and tie or suit dress.

21. Has an inherent love for new ideas

Positive: Their ideas or not, the INTP thrives on innovation and loves to see the world get shaken up again and again by new concepts that push boundaries. Their admiration and appreciation for such creativity shows as they support fledgling scientists or writers who need advocates, back the political leader with the greatest track record of change and try to live a life that isn't stuck in superstition and outdated traditions.

Negative: Sometimes the INTP can get so bogged down in their mind-consuming pursuit of new ideas that they miss what is right in front of their eyes. Not all traditions are bad – some have endured not because they hold people down while propping up others, but because they are simply based on good ideas. But it can feel as though the INTP would like to change things just for the sake of novelty, bypassing their normally on-point sense of logic.

In Relationships: Once an INTP has thrown him or herself into a love match, they have a natural ability to keep things interesting. This can include never-before-tried activities, new restaurants with exotic cuisine or spontaneous trips to far-flung countries. If the relationship hits a rough patch, INTPs are also open-minded enough to embrace nontraditional forms of therapy; whatever it takes to keep their relationship together, the INTP is willing to try it, no dragged feet or resentful eye-rolling.

At Work: INTPs in the workplace can be annoying – annoying because they are always coming up with awesome ideas to replace the stale old ones (oh the envy their coworkers feel!). But INTPs can also appreciate someone else's great concept, and if they can, they will champion it to whoever will listen. Positive change that improves upon the old ways is the INTP's calling card, as they seek to better their own environment and the environments of others.

22. Enjoys sharing new concepts and theories with others

Positive: No one likes a hoarder, and that goes not only for physical objects, but ideas as well. That's why the INTP is so great – they love new ideas and theories and they equally love talking about them with others, particularly people who are at the same level of expertise (but any enthusiastic conversationalist will do). It's one of the ways that INTPs can break out of their normally introverted shell – get them talking about the latest scientific breakthroughs and watch their eyes light up.

Negative: The drawback is that not everyone is interested in the same, rather esoteric, topics that INTPs are drawn toward, so that person next to them on the subway or standing in line behind them at the grocery store may find themselves stuck in a conversation on a topic about which they know – and care – nothing. Intellectual topics are incredibly appealing to INTPs, but they're in a rather limited class.

In Relationships: If INTPs can find romantic partners who match them intellectually, then these couples will have plenty to talk about for the rest of their lives. Casual observers at the table next to theirs at the restaurant might not understand a single word of their technical or scientific jargon, but the INTP who can bounce new concepts and theories off their beloved will see stars in their eyes for decades.

At Work: INTPs are interesting in the workplace, because while they prefer to work independently and without the constant interference of coworkers or higher-ups, they are born brain-stormers. It's true they generally believe their ideas are the best, but they have the broad intelligence to recognize a great theory, even when it isn't their own. INTPs might not like collaborating on projects, but they know the adage about two heads being better than one is true.

23. Finds no joy or pleasure in routine tasks

Positive: By denouncing the need for routine tasks – those daily doings in life that constitute a total time suck – INTPs free themselves up for a great many other things – things that include coming up with brilliant new ideas that can be turned into advances in science or technology or more creative, artistic endeavors that make the world a better place. The INTP never loses sight of his or her passions and focuses on the activities that utilize their great potential.

Negative: On the debit side of this equation, however, INTPs can become incredibly lax in normal, everyday upkeep of both their home and their person. They might let the dishes pile up in the sink for a few weeks or go an inordinate period of time without clipping their nails – stuff the rest of us do when it needs to be done, but which the INTP finds incredibly boring and quarrelsome, a total intrusion on their precious time and efforts.

In Relationships: INTPs' partners put up with a lot of eccentricities from their mates, and while the trade-off is worth it, it can still be totally maddening when the INTP won't stop to change the toilet paper roll if it runs out or avoids walking the dog as much as possible. A compromise must be made (or a maid must be hired), because part of being an adult is doing things you don't enjoy. You just have to learn to suck it up and do them.

At Work: INTPs like exciting, dynamic careers where they are always being challenged, and their dislike for mundane, routine tasks keeps these personality types out of cubicles for the most part. It can also keep them from pursuing management positions, because a great deal of routine responsibility accompanies the positions of authority – and INTPs are happiest both when no one is telling them what to do and they don't have to tell anyone else.

24. Tolerant and flexible when it comes to most situations

Positive: In today's rapidly evolving social climate, tolerance is the key to peace – and to progress. INTPs occupy the seemingly paradoxical position of being "dreamy logicians" – they hope for the better world of tomorrow because it makes sense to promote peace and equality and tolerance. And they are flexible in both mind and lifestyle: open to new ideas and comfortable adapting to whatever changes or challenges that life throws their way. Live and let live, INTP.

Negative: Coupled with their discomfort when it comes to expressing emotion, the INTP can actually get railroaded by more forceful personalities, so that even though they are uneasy about something – you might see them turn bright red as they realize their values are being compromised and ignored – they just don't have it in them to speak up right away; they will wait until the hurt or anger has been bottled so long that they explode.

In Relationships: INTPs could actually do well dating each other, because their aforementioned loathing for chores is the same, along with their similar easy-going approach to finally getting it done. That is, neither party is going to harp on the other for not picking up wet towels from the floor. This personality trait is also good for parents, because anyone with kids knows that the best laid plans of mice and men oft go astray...

At Work: The only way you can really get on the INTP's nerves at work is if you keep bugging him or her while they are trying to work in peaceful independence. Other than that, they are excellent coworkers, generous with what they can endure, and they are great employees, the kind of people who can be counted on to handle a last-minute assignment that needs to be completed with swift turnaround.

25. Reserved or shy around people they have never met

Positive: Reservation or shyness around people that the INTP have never met before is not them being antisocial or snobby (which is how it can be perceived); it is simply the INTP's way of keeping people at a distance until they have decided if anyone is trustworthy enough to come closer. INTPs might not be in the mix, befriending everyone, but that actually lessens their chances of making a bad snap judgment about someone and letting a manipulator into their lives.

Negative: Shyness and a more retiring personality in public can also mean missed opportunities – positive ones, especially since the INTP is so enthusiastic about sharing ideas. If they never speak up, then someone who has the exact same interests as them will never find out, and what could have been a fantastic connection never takes off. If INTPs work a little harder to be heard or noticed around people they don't know, they might end up surprised with the results.

In Relationships: You've heard it before: "I had no idea so-and-so was into me – he/she was always so quiet!" Sometimes when it comes to love, we have to step outside of our comfort zone and put ourselves out there. INTPs will likely find kindred spirits in their introverted brethren, but how will anyone make a connection if neither party can overcome their reserve long enough to make eye contact and say hello?

At Work: INTPs don't naturally make friends easily on the job, unless the conditions are just right, and this is definitely one of those areas where their shyness, coupled with their quiet self-confidence, can be misconstrued as arrogance by coworkers, especially if the INTP is the new employee. In many instances, though, their brilliance and their integrity will speak for them and the more INTPs work with the same core group, the more they will open up.

26. Self-confident and gregarious around people they know

Positive: You walk into a bar and are immediately drawn to the infectious laughter of someone who appears to be the life of the party, surrounded by friends. If you were to run into that person at a more straight-laced work event, and they're an INTP, then you would see a completely different person. INTPs might seem as though they have split personalities, but their confidence and gregariousness is something like a reward for the people who have stuck around and become close.

Negative: This means that those who don't know the INTP that well – those who aren't in the inner circle – can feel pretty frozen-out by this personality type. If they see the INTP with friends and see the way they interact with bubbly cheer and wit, it can make them feel pretty bad that the INTP doesn't consider them to be close enough to let them be a part of that side.

In Relationships: The INTP at home can be a far cry from the guy or gal in the workplace or even out grocery shopping. In comfortable surroundings, with the person they love, their wit, their playfulness and their charm really comes out, so that the INTP's mate is reminded every day why they are together. And they'll get used to having their partner clam up again in public, though it might be jarring at first.

At Work: The shy INTP on the first day of a new job will, if they are lucky, eventually assimilate to their surroundings and their coworkers and show that more fun, humorous side to the people with whom they spend long hours each day. As long as they are comfortable, coworkers can expect the INTP to be fairly sociable, excited to share ideas, willing to help others and – who knows – they might even start looking forward to lunch break with the work crew.

27. Has trouble understanding others' feelings

Positive: It might not seem as though this is a positive trait, but there are lot of decisions in life that are best made from an objective point of view. Separating feeling from logic is not something that INTPs tend to grapple with, the way so many of us do, and so INTPs are capable of making some of the most incredibly difficult choices. Let's face it: we make wrong choices all the time because of our hearts, and it ends up worse for everyone in the end.

Negative: Unfortunately, understanding where other people are coming from – comprehending how they feel or how your actions will make them feel – is a social skill that comes in handy for more than just the "big choices." And with INTPs deploying their logic instead, they can come across as incredibly rude, insensitive and even heartless. If that goes on for too long, they might start to earn a reputation that precedes them, which closes avenues and opportunities.

In Relationships: Again, INTPs have a lot to offer their partners, but a wealth of emotional understanding is not one of those things. Unless the INTP is dating a personality replica of themselves, they are going to be met with genuine shock and horror when their partners realize how little the INTP can comprehend when it comes to matters of the heart. A long life of patience and sincerity with the right person, though, can help the INTP to hone their emotional intelligence.

At Work: The INTP is undoubtedly brilliant and a hard worker, and they will more likely than not end up making friends with their coworkers, but their lack of emotional intelligence can leave those with whom they work in close quarters rather baffled and sometimes a bit hurt. INTPs will have to work hard all their lives to be more considerate of others and to stop and think about other people's feelings.

28. Can be abrupt at times

Positive: When you have as many ideas as the INTP does, whirling through their minds at all times, it's difficult to stay focused on one topic for too long. This is why the INTP can came across as abrupt, especially to people who don't know them very well, and it's not just changing subjects – sometimes it's ending conversations or even beginning new ones. What this means, though, is that INTPs are always pushing for progress and trying to move things forward, toward improvement.

Negative: Many people would prefer to finish a conversation or a project before moving onto something else, and it can be jarring for them when they come into contact with the INTP, who is rip-roaring and ready to go, onto the next thing. This is definitely one of the traits that makes INTPs difficult to get close to, as it is terribly off-putting for a lot of people to feel as though their chat has been rudely cut off.

In Relationships: Partners of INTPs can work with their mates to get them to be less abrupt, but it is one of those traits that will likely never go away – so finding a middle ground is the best course of action. On the other hand, if INTPs find an equally abrupt partner, they can spend their lives together, happily skipping from idea to idea or activity to activity – perceiving types will be prone to this sort of behavior.

At Work: Whether it's a sharp comment at a coworker or the INTP standing up in the middle of presentation to get a drink of water (and really, seeing nothing wrong with it), their abruptness can be a bit of a liability in the workplace. Yet it is also a trait which ensures that the INTP can be counted on to change direction comfortably and with greater flexibility than other personality types.

29. Can be overly critical or sarcastic oward other people

Positive: Let's face it: some people need to be told what's what. And the INTP, who doesn't often speak up in this fashion, will be the one to do it if it really has to be done – and they will do it with a sharpness that leaves people breathless. INTPs really love sarcasm, too, and it especially amuses them when others don't pick up on it. It's not for everyone, but those who appreciate it can see that INTPs do it so well.

Negative: A lot of us in this world get by by being as nice as possible to others. INTPs aren't naturally forgiving people, and their sarcasm – almost always deployed when they are saying something critical – can be grating, obnoxious and even downright rude if they let themselves go. It's a shame, because they are good people to get to know, but it's hard to get past that rough shell on the outside – the one that seems so impossibly mean-spirited at times.

In Relationships: INTPs are the type who don't like to do their dishes, but then they'll turn around and critique how their partners do it. Frustrating? Absolutely. So what the INTP really needs is someone who calls them out when they are being brats, someone with a stiff backbone and a stiff upper lip. INTPs prefer that type of partner anyway, but their mates can't be shy about shutting them down when their criticism is misplaced.

At Work: Coworkers are bound to feel the sting of the INTP now and then, but like the romantic partners of this personality type, they have to learn to stand up to them and put them in their place. INTPs are so naturally intelligent and think quite highly of themselves, to the point where they can forget that they aren't perfect themselves, especially at work. All it takes is one person to tell them to knock it off, though, and they'll get the picture.

30. Often misunderstood by others due to their demeanor

Positive: If everyone can read you like a book, there's no mystery. And the INTP, whether they realize it or not, are usually shrouded in a kind of mystery (certainly, someone seeing them with friends they know well and then at a party where they don't know anyone would wonder how someone can be so different). Because INTPs come across as aloof, a little arrogant and sometimes shy, this misunderstanding makes them interesting to the outside world.

Negative: But being misunderstood by the majority of people they meet can be incredibly frustrating for INTPs, who have a lot to offer the world if they could just get people on the same page as them. This frustration, in turn, can make them turn even further inward, creating a vicious cycle of misunderstanding and retreat, over and over, until the INTP is downright depressed.

In Relationships: Letting someone in is difficult enough, but INTPs have to find people they want to share their lives with first and foremost. If potential mates are misunderstanding them left and right, their dating pool is getting a lot smaller by the second. However, when INTPs finally find their matches, the veil is slowly lifted and their partners will likely be pleasantly surprised by all the good stuff that's lurking underneath once they are better understood.

At Work: Being misunderstood by their coworkers, boss or even clients can be difficult for the INTP, who just wants to achieve, succeed and defy expectations – all without taking their personality into account. But social skills are an important part of any job, and if the INTP wants to be heard, they will have to make the changes necessary to ensure that people are turning their ears toward them – and not away.

31. Fiercely independent

Positive: INTPs might not have much use for balancing a checkbook or dusting their living room, but these types of personalities are pioneers, born and bred. They don't want anyone taking care of them and they delight in self-sufficiency and in the knowledge that at the end of the day, they only have themselves to answer to. Associates of INTPs never have to worry about this type asking them for awkward favors or dragging them along to dull social events.

Negative: Everyone, no matter how independent or self-sufficient, needs help at some point. For the INTP, asking for help even at their most desperate moment, is a terrible blow to their self-confidence. Yet the pride that keeps them from letting others give them a hand when they need it can hold them back and keep them down. INTPs have to learn that it's okay to take the aid of others – it doesn't make them weak.

In Relationships: Fiercely independent partners can be tough to acclimate to, especially if the INTP's mate had a more cozy, loving idea of relationship in mind, but the major upside to this trait is that, in the event of a break-up, the INTP won't feel the loss quite as deeply as someone who has invested their entire life into the commitment. INTPs are not only resilient, they are practical, even in matters of the heart.

At Work: Independence plays a huge role in the types of careers that INTPs gravitate toward. If they have to work in a more structured setting, like an office or a laboratory, they will choose an environment where each individual has a great deal of autonomy over their day. INTPs also favor freelance positions, which gives them the ultimate control over their days and allows them to work when they're feeling inspired and accomplish other things when they are not.

32. Thinks in unconventional and off-beat ways

Positive: Where would any of us be if Benjamin Franklin hadn't gone outside during a thunderstorm with a kite? What if the Wright brothers hadn't dreamed of flight? INTPs are born to innovate, because they dare to focus not on what has already been achieved, but about what could be possible in the future. The world needs people who get looked at funny, who get laughed out of conferences, who get doors slammed in their faces – these are the people who affect change.

Negative: Sometimes, though, because the INTP is so caught up in his or her own mind, their unconventional thinking can surpass off-beat and veer into nonsensical and even crazy. Occasionally, the harder they try to drive forward, the more push-back they'll receive. INTPs have to learn to make their ideas more palatable to wider audiences, or they risk not being taken seriously, and all of their genius will go to naught.

In Relationships: Though they can be severe and critical, a romantic life shared with the INTP is never boring, because underneath all the hard-nosed sarcasm is an adventurous soul who loves to experiment and push boundaries. It's there, lurking under the surface, and it's waiting for the right partner to come along and unearth all the eccentric fun.

At Work: Scientists, mathematicians, doctors, even professors – they all seem pretty straight-laced, but surprisingly, off-beat, experimental and unconventional modes of thinking serve these types of professionals well, and it's why INTPs can often be found in these careers, flourishing. INTPs are exceptionally gifted when it comes to taking known and established fact and pushing it one step further. They're the sort who use the scientific method and end up proving some uncanny medical theory that saves thousands of lives.

33. Not concerned with traditional social values like security or popularity

Positive: A lot of people never reach their full potential because they are afraid of what other people will think. They don't want to step on toes; they don't want to ruffle feathers. If there is one thing that can be said for INTPs, it's that they would rather be doing what they love and being happy than conforming to what others think of as "normal" or "desirable." If more people lived like this, the world would be a much less grumpy place.

Negative: When we live and work in the wider world, we sign an unspoken social contract. INTPs try to pretend that they never affixed their signature, and sometimes they take the notion of their own personal sovereignty to extremes, truly offending good people who deserve respect and consideration. Just because they don't care if they're liked, INTPs don't have the right to stomp on other people's happiness.

In Relationships: No gold diggers need apply to the INTP's love boat, because this personality type does not give one hoot if they make millions or end up famous and beloved by the world. But it can be somewhat exasperating for the INTP's partner if the INTP is always pursuing their latest passion, while everyone else is putting down roots.

At Work: INTPs might make a decent living accidentally, but they don't pursue any line of work just because it pays well.

Equally, they don't mind if they aren't voted Best Office Friend, as long as their work is appreciated. INTPs often blend their professional pursuits with their passions, so while most parents would prefer that their children consider security and stability as they grow up, INTPs continue to march to the beat of their own drummer.